Elizabeth Blackwell

THE FIRST WOMAN DOCTOR

Elizabeth Blackwell

THE FIRST WOMAN DOCTOR

by Francene Sabin
illustrated by Ann Toulmin-Rothe

Troll Associates

Library of Congress Cataloging in Publication Data

Sabin, Francene.
    Elizabeth Blackwell, the first woman doctor.

    Summary: Traces the early life of the first woman
physician, relating the struggles women had to face in
becoming doctors and practicing medicine.
    1. Blackwell, Elizabeth, 1821-1910—Juvenile
literature.   2. Physicians—New York (State)—Biography.
3. Women physicians—New York (State)—Biography.
[1. Blackwell, Elizabeth, 1821-1910.   2. Physicians.
3. Women physicians]   I. Toulmin-Rothe, Ann, ill.
II. Title.
R154.B623S2   610'.92'4 [B]   81-23140
ISBN 0-89375-756-X   AACR2
ISBN 0-89375-757-8 (pbk.)

Elizabeth Blackwell

THE FIRST WOMAN DOCTOR

Six-year-old Elizabeth Blackwell sat on the dark, well-polished stairs. Peeking between the stair railings, she could see down into the brightly lit parlor. Mama sat in a dainty lady's chair. She was mending the lace trim on a shawl.

Papa Blackwell stood at the fireplace, warming his hands. Elizabeth thought he looked very handsome in his elegant white suit. Mr. Blackwell wore a white suit to business, no matter what season it was. He was the owner of a sugar refinery, and his white suit stood for the clean, pure white sugar produced by his company.

The only times Mr. Blackwell wore a dark suit were to attend church on Sunday, and when he went to parties or political meetings. Then, like other proper Englishmen of the 1820s, he wore a black wool coat, dark-gray trousers, and a gray-and-black striped tie. Elizabeth thought he looked important in his dark clothes. But she liked his everyday white suits even more.

From where she sat on the stairs, Elizabeth could not see her Aunt Barbara. But she could hear her voice quite clearly. As usual, Aunt Barbara was complaining about Elizabeth.

"She can be a most difficult child," Barbara Blackwell said. "Anna and Marianne are such polite little ladies. They are always good and do as they are told. In my opinion, Elizabeth is far too strong-willed and independent for a girl. It's a pity she wasn't born a boy!"

"To my mind," said Mr. Blackwell, "those are fine qualities for a girl. I think no less of my daughters than I do of my baby son, Sam. And if God blesses us with more children, it is the same to me if they are boys or girls."

Barbara sighed heavily. "Your feelings are noble, Brother Samuel. But I fear the results," she said. "What possible use can young ladies make of Latin, Greek, history, and mathematics? A lady need know only a bit of art and music, embroidery, some French, and how to conduct herself properly."

"You must be fair, Barbara," said Mrs. Blackwell in her soft voice. "Anna and Marianne, as you said yourself, are very good little girls. As for Elizabeth, she has a special spark. I am sure she will do great things."

Great things, Elizabeth repeated to herself. *Oh, indeed I shall.* And in her mind the six-year-old pictured herself on a big, white horse, leading an army into battle, and then as the captain of a tall-masted ship, sailing into a storm-tossed sea. Then she imagined herself putting the last strokes of paint onto a huge canvas, while a crowd of people cheered the great artist. Then she saw herself healing hundreds of sad, sick children, making those sad faces smile brightly.

"Doctor Blackwell," she said aloud. "That sounds *so* good."

Elizabeth yawned. She got up and tiptoed back to her room. A few moments later she was in bed and fast asleep.

Though she did not know it, Elizabeth Blackwell, born on February 3, 1821, was being raised in a most unusual way. At that time in Bristol, England, where the Blackwells lived, girls were given very little education. Most people felt that girls were not as smart as boys, not as important, and not as able to do most things as well as boys.

Women were not allowed to become doctors, lawyers, bankers, or to hold any other important position. Women could work as house servants, in factories, in taverns, or on farms. But every penny they earned became the property of their fathers or husbands or brothers. However, if they were not very poor, women were expected to stay home and be "ladies."

13

Samuel Blackwell did not think the way other men did. He believed that there was no such thing as "man's work." He felt that women were as smart and able as men, and that little girls should be as well educated as little boys.

Samuel Blackwell was different in other ways, too. Many well-to-do-English people ignored the injustices of the world. Not Samuel. He fought against the slave trade that sent black people from Africa to the United States and the British colonies. He was against child labor, which put five- and six-year-olds to work in the coal mines and cloth mills. He was against wages so low that workers and their families starved to death on them. And he made these feelings very clear to all of his children.

Elizabeth's father was a kind, fair, and loving man. He never spanked his children. In those days, a naughty child was whipped or beaten, locked up in a room with no food, and punished in other ways. People believed that harshness was the only way to "drive the devil" out of children who misbehaved. Mr. Blackwell thought this was a horrible attitude. Not only did he not punish his children, he could even say "no" to them in a loving way.

One time, the girls wanted to climb out an upstairs window of their house and sit on a small, slanted roof. There, they would be able to see all of Bristol and even some of the far-off countryside through Anna's small telescope. But first they had to get permission from their father.

"I will ask Papa," said Elizabeth, who was nicknamed "Bessie."

"No, let me," said Marianne. Marianne's nickname was "Polly."

"I am the oldest," said Anna. "We shall make up a proper request in writing, and *I* shall take it to Papa."

Anna had the neatest handwriting, and she was the best writer. So Polly and Bessie voted to go along with her decision. Soon the note was written and handed to Mr. Blackwell. His answer, given to the girls that night, was a poem.

Anna, Bessie, and Polly,
Your request is mere folly,
The roof is too high
For those who can't fly.
If I let you go there,
I suppose your next prayer
Will be for a hop
To the chimney top!
So I charge you, three misses,
Not to show your faces
On parapet wall
Or chimney so tall,
But to keep on the earth,
The place of your birth.

And that, with a laugh, was the last word on the subject. But it wasn't the end of poetic answers in the Blackwell house. Another time, young Cousin Maria came to spend a few weeks with the Blackwells. The guest room, where she slept, was large and very dark and had a large four-poster bed. Maria was scared to sleep in this strange, big room. So, each night Anna and Polly took turns sleeping with her. Elizabeth wanted to take a turn, too. But her sisters said she was "too little."

"The bed is so big," said Elizabeth, offering a solution to the problem, "that all four of us can sleep in it."

"Oh, what a fine idea," squealed Maria.

The girls all agreed, and they wrote a note to Mr. Blackwell, asking permission.

His answer was another poem:

If you four girls were together to lie
I fear you'd resemble the pigs in their sty!
Such groaning!! Such gruntings!!!
  Such sprawling about!!!!
I could not allow such confusion and
  rout!!!!!
So this is my judgment: 'Tis wisdom you'll
  own
Two *beds for* four *girls are far better*
  than one!

There was a lot of love and happiness in the home of Samuel Blackwell. But there was sadness, as well. Mr. and Mrs. Blackwell always wanted a large family. And almost every year Mrs. Blackwell gave birth to a baby. As often as not, however, the baby did not live. Before little Sam was born, there had been two other baby boys in the Blackwell family. Both had died before they reached two months of age.

It was even worse in other families. Elizabeth had one aunt who gave birth to eight boys and lost all eight of them. It did not matter whether a family was rich or poor. There were not many doctors, and there were no medicines and no cures for most sicknesses.

Every time a baby died in her family, Elizabeth felt the house fill with unhappiness. Her mother would be gloomy for weeks. Her father would sit and sigh with deep sadness. Elizabeth, who was very close to her father, felt terrible.

"Papa, why doesn't anybody help babies to live?" she asked him one day. "Why isn't there someone to take care of all the sick people? It's wrong, the way things are."

"Yes, Bessie," he said, stroking her hair gently. "There are many things wrong with this world, and we must do everything in our power to set them right."

Elizabeth's mouth set in a hard, straight line. "When I grow up, I shall be a doctor," she said. "I shall help babies to live and children to stay healthy and —"

"—and if anyone can do it," Mr. Blackwell said, picking up her sentence, "you can. You are a very clever and good little lady. If you study hard and really believe you can do it, nothing can stop you."

That night, as eight-year-old Elizabeth lay in her bed, she thought, "Papa says I can be anything I want, and he is a very smart man. So he must be right!"

Elizabeth *did* study hard. There were many books in the house, and she read every one. Each year, at Christmas, the Blackwell children put together a small book of their own poems and stories. This would be their present for Mr. Blackwell. It was always easy to tell which ones his Bessie had written. They were very serious and done in carefully printed letters. Like everything else Elizabeth did, her papers had to be just right—no matter how long it took!

At lessons, with Eliza Major, the children's governess, Elizabeth was always the best pupil.

The others might want to run outside and play before "school-time" was over. Never Elizabeth. She wanted Miss Major to give her more and more work. She was the same with all the tutors who gave lessons to the Blackwell children. Elizabeth was never bored with learning and doing new things.

None of the children went to a school. Instead, they learned from the tutors who came to the house. There were no schools in England where girls could study serious subjects. Being tutored was the only way for them to be educated.

There were good schools for boys in Bristol. But these schools were only for members of the church of England. The Blackwells were members of the Independent church, a religious group like the Quakers. Because of their religious beliefs, the Blackwell boys could not attend the better schools in Bristol.

In those days, boys and girls did not have classes together—or even spend much time together. But since there were no schools for them, the Blackwell children did most things together. This was the normal way of life for their family. The boys and girls were treated equally at lessons, at play, at the dinner table—in just about every way possible.

Years later, when Elizabeth was a medical student, she would remember the boy-girl equality at home. And so, when her classmates —all young men—teased her, she just laughed it off. They might have felt strange to be in a class with a young woman. But Elizabeth was used to having boys as classmates. Often, their teasing reminded her of her brothers.

For a long time, Mr. Blackwell's sugar business was very successful. And the family lived quite well. There was plenty of money for the big house in Bristol, and the summer house in the country—for servants and for tutors, for Mr. and Mrs. Blackwell and their eight children—

31

and to support Mr. Blackwell's four sisters—
who lived with them—and every other friend or
relation who needed money.

Then, at the beginning of 1832, things
changed. The sugar plant started losing money.
Mr. Blackwell lost more money in bad
investments. Suddenly, the family was not rich.
And Mr. Blackwell made a decision.

"We are going to America," he announced one
evening.

"Why must we leave England?" asked young
Sam.

"For many reasons," said Mr. Blackwell.
"There, you will be able to go to school. That is
something you cannot do here. And America is
a land of freedom, new ideas, opportunity for
all." He seemed to look right at Elizabeth as he
spoke.

Mr. Blackwell went on, giving more reasons,
and explaining his feelings. Then he asked
everyone how they felt about the move. When
all the talking was done, only Aunt Ann refused

to go. The others immediately began making plans for the start of a new life in the New World.

Once the decision was made, nothing could change Mr. Blackwell's mind. Not even when a group of Bristol merchants begged him to stay. They offered to lend him any amount of money he needed. And, they said, he could pay it back whenever he wanted to. Mr. Blackwell was very grateful for this kind offer. Even so, he told the merchants, the Blackwells were leaving for America that summer.

34

On a bright August morning in 1832, the *Cosmo,* her sails billowing in the wind, left England with the Blackwells aboard. The seven weeks and four days that followed were a living nightmare. More than two hundred people were crowded aboard the ship. Most of them were steerage passengers—packed like cattle in the filthy, rat-infested blackness far below decks.

Even for first-class passengers, like the Blackwells, the trip was miserable. Six or more people were crammed into each "good" cabin. The portholes leaked, water soaked everything, and chill winds blew through the cabins day and night.

Elizabeth was seasick for much of the voyage. But that was nothing compared to the suffering of many others aboard the *Cosmo.* Below decks, there was an outbreak of cholera. This disease, caused by unsanitary living conditions, claimed many lives among the steerage passengers.

During the final days of the voyage, Elizabeth was strangely quiet. She would stand on deck, staring out over the water. One day, her father said, "Are you homesick, Bessie? Are you afraid of what lies ahead in America?"

Elizabeth shook her head. "No, I am sad about what is happening on this ship," she said. "Yesterday I heard Captain Gillespie say that it was a good crossing. He thinks it good because not everyone in steerage has cholera, and that more than half of them are still alive. How can that be good? I think it is the most frightful thing I have ever heard."

"But there is cholera on every ocean voyage," Mr. Blackwell said.

"Why *must* it be that way?" Elizabeth demanded. "Why *must* we think all those deaths are normal? It's wrong, Papa! I think we have to prevent diseases, like cholera and smallpox and the others. There have to be doctors who show people how to stay well, and to help them when they do get sick. That is what I want to do when I am older!"

Soon after the *Cosmo* reached the United States in October 1832, the Blackwells settled into a house in New York City. Not long after that, Mr. Blackwell became deeply involved in anti-slavery activities. Many meetings were held in the Blackwell house.

Elizabeth met William Lloyd Garrison, the editor of the *Liberator,* a newspaper devoted to ending slavery. Other visitors she came to know were Dr. Lyman Beecher, the famous minister, and his daughter, Harriet Beecher Stowe, who would one day write *Uncle Tom's Cabin.* She also met Horace Mann, the great educator, and Ralph Waldo Emerson, the noted writer.

The twelve-year-old girl was getting a very rare education just by living in that house. The visitors she spoke with included many of America's finest thinkers. Their words and deeds would change America. Among other things, these were the people who organized the underground railroad, which was used to smuggle slaves to safety. They also fought against child labor and the unfair treatment of women.

As she listened to these people, Elizabeth's faith in herself grew stronger. And she needed this faith. She knew that no medical school had ever accepted a female student. In fact, women were not welcome into *any* college. But Elizabeth had her mind set on changing this. No matter how long it took or how hard she had to work, she was going to become a doctor.

The next five years were busy ones for Elizabeth. When she wasn't in high school herself, she was helping her sisters Anna and Marianne to teach others. The three sisters had set up a small school for black children, who could not get an education any other way. And when several of her brothers and sisters fell ill with a severe fever, Elizabeth nursed them back to health.

At first, Mr. Blackwell's sugar business did well in New York. Then it began to lose money. And problems came one after another. A fire raged through his sugar refinery, destroying everything but the four walls. Then a bank failure wiped out most of Mr. Blackwell's savings. And through it all his health began to fail.

Because he hoped things would be better in a new place, Mr. Blackwell moved the family to Cincinnati, Ohio. There, he planned to start the first sugar refinery west of the Allegheny Mountains. And there, too, his health would improve. But it was not to be. Soon after the family arrived in Cincinnati, Mr. Blackwell's illness worsened. Within a few months he was dead.

Mrs. Blackwell, left with nine children and no money, showed great strength. She called the family together and said, "We shall start a small school. Anna, Marianne, and Elizabeth will be its teachers. Samuel and Henry will go to all the houses and tell people of the school. Emily, Ellen, Howard, and George will be good children, and help in any way they can."

Running the school was hard work, but it paid for their food and housing. Elizabeth put in long hours of teaching, even though she was impatient to get on with her plans for the future.

Elizabeth gave every free moment to her own studies. Since her father's death, she had become even more serious about medicine. Now the teenager began reading and learning from every medical book she could find. She asked questions of any doctor willing to speak with a woman about medicine. But even those who answered her questions tried to discourage her from trying to become a doctor.

"No medical school on earth will have you," said one doctor. "It is ridiculous...unthinkable... impossible!"

Elizabeth did not give up. She wrote a letter to Dr. Abraham Cox, who had been the Blackwell's family physician in New York. He was the first doctor to encourage her. He sent her the names of medical schools and told her how to apply to them. But he warned her not to raise her hopes very high.

For the next few years Elizabeth continued to teach and study books about medicine. At the same time, she applied to one medical school after another. Not one would accept her. Then, in October of 1847, she received a letter of acceptance from Geneva Medical College in New York State. She was overjoyed. In almost no time her bags were packed, and she was on a train heading for school.

44

It was only when she arrived there that
Elizabeth learned the hardest months and years
were still to come. There were teachers who
hated her, and teachers who would not let her
into their classrooms. Fellow students mocked
her, insulted her, even threatened her. But,

more determined than ever, she completed her studies and graduated with high honors. She was, at last, the first woman doctor in the world!

In the years that followed, Dr. Elizabeth Blackwell blazed new trails in medicine. In addition to setting an example for other women seeking careers in medicine, she established a hospital and clinic called the New York Infirmary for Women and Children. She also founded a medical school for women, helped to train nurses for duty in the Civil War, and wrote many books on health and the prevention of disease.

Not only was Elizabeth Blackwell the first woman doctor, she was also first in many other ways. Long before most other doctors saw the importance of cleanliness and proper diet, Dr. Blackwell was showing people why these things were so important. She called it "preventive medicine," saying that "even better than curing ills is seeing that ills do not happen in the first place."

Elizabeth Blackwell never forgot all the needless infant deaths she had seen when she was a girl—or the cholera epidemic aboard the ship that brought her to America. She gave her whole life to fighting ignorance and illness. And when she died in 1910, at the age of 89, Dr. Elizabeth Blackwell had written a shining chapter in the history of medicine—and humanity.